TACKLING
SELF-ASSESSMENT

CONSUMERS' ASSOCIATION

Which? Books are commissioned and researched by
Consumers' Association and published by
Which? Ltd,
2 Marylebone Road, London NW1 4DF
Email address: books@which.net

Distributed by The Penguin Group:
Penguin Books Ltd, 27 Wrights Lane, London W8 5TZ

First edition June 1998
Copyright © 1998 Which? Ltd

British Library Cataloguing in Publication Data
A catalogue record for this book is available from the British
Library

ISBN 0 85202 721 4

Tackling Self-assessment was abridged by Anthony Bailey from
the *Which? Tax Saving Guide 1998*

For a full list of Which? books, please write to Which? Books,
Castlemead, Gascoyne Way, Hertford X, SG14 1LH
or access our website at www.which.net

Cartoons and cover illustration by David Pattison,
Cartoon Partnership
Cover design by Creation Communications
Typeset by Saxon Graphics Ltd, Derby
Printed and bound in Great Britain by St Edmundsbury Press,
Bury St Edmunds

CONTENTS

	Introduction	7
1	Filling in your tax return	11
2	Checking your income tax	21
3	Income from a job or pension	29
4	Tax on your fringe benefits	37
5	Working for yourself	47
6	At home with tax	59
7	You and your family	66
8	Splitting up and maintenance	71
9	Tax for older people	77
10	Dealing with the Inland Revenue	81
	Index	91

INTRODUCTION

You could be one of the nine million people sent a tax return each year – if you are self-employed or an employee paying higher-rate tax or you have some sort of income that isn't taxed before you receive it. The tax return deals with income tax, capital gains tax and (for some people) National Insurance. Knowing how your tax bill is worked out can save you pounds.

Some income can be tax-free, for example, income from TESSAs and PEPs and some social security benefits, and allowances make otherwise 'taxable' income tax-free. Everyone gets a basic personal allowance. You

may also be entitled to extra allowances if you're married or if you or your spouse are over 65.

You may also qualify for tax-allowable deductions – for example, contributions to pension schemes or some payments to charity. Certain expenses can be deducted. The deductions and expenses you can claim depend on the relevant 'schedule' of rules. For example, schedule E deals with income from an employer, schedule D with income from self-employment, schedule A with income from letting a property.

Inventing expenses and claiming allowances fraudulently or concealing income or gains is tax evasion – a criminal offence. But arranging your affairs in a way that legally reduces your tax bill is fair play.

Tax facts and timetable for the 1997-8 tax year (6 April 1997 to 5 April 1998)

(Note: figures in italics are those announced in the March 1998 Budget; they will apply to the 1998–9 tax year.)

- Everybody gets a tax-free personal allowance of £4,045 *(£4,195)*.
- The married couple's allowance is £1,830 *(£1,900)*. It gives 'restricted relief'– all eligible taxpayers receive 15 per cent of £1,830, i.e. £274.50. This is deducted from your tax bill.
- People aged 65 and over can get a personal allowance of £5,220 *(£5,410)* or £5,400 *(£5,600)* at the age of 75, and an increased married couple's allowance of £3,185 *(£3,305)* which rises to £3,225

(£3,345) at 75. The extra allowances are reduced if total income exceeds £15,600 *(£16,200)*.

- You pay 20 per cent (lower rate) income tax on the first £4,100 *(£4,300)* of taxable income.
- You pay 23 per cent (basic rate) income tax on taxable income between £4,101 and £26,100 *(£4,301 and £27,100)*, except that on most taxable savings and investment income up to £26,100 *(£27,100)* you pay 20 per cent income tax.
- You pay 40 per cent (higher rate) income tax above £26,100 *(£27,100)*.
- You don't pay capital gains on the first £6,500 *(£6,800)* of chargeable gains. Above this, you normally pay tax at your highest income tax rate.
- You don't pay inheritance tax on the first £215,000 *(£223,000)* of a taxable estate. Above this, you may be taxed at up to 40 per cent.

By 31 January 1998

- 1996-7 tax returns must be sent back.
- Remaining tax for 1996-7 due.
- Taxpayers who pay on account must make the first payment on account for 1997-8 tax year.

April 1998

- Tax returns for 1997-8 tax year despatched.

By 31 May 1998

- P60s issued to employees and to pensioners receiving an income from a previous employer's pension scheme or private pension plan – the P60 gives details of your taxable pay and tax paid for 1997-8.

By 6 July 1998

- P11Ds issued to employees and directors earning £8,500 or more and receiving fringe benefits and/or expenses – the P11D gives details of your taxable fringe benefits and expenses for tax year 1997-8.

By 31 July 1998

- Taxpayers who pay on account must make the second payment on account for 1997-8 tax year.

By 30 September 1998

- Send back tax return if you want your tax office to work out your bill before the payment deadline of 31 January 1999 and/or if you want underpayments of tax of up to £1,000 to be collected by PAYE.

By 5 October 1998

- People who haven't received a tax return must tell their tax office about any taxable income or capital gain which has not already been taxed in full.

By 31 January 1998

- 1997-8 tax returns must be sent back.
- Remaining tax for 1997-8 due.
- Taxpayers who pay on account must make first payment on account for tax year 1998-9.
- The Revenue must tell you by now if it intends to start an enquiry into your 1996-7 return.

FILLING IN YOUR TAX RETURN

1

The 1997-8 tax return asks for information on income, allowable deductions and allowances applicable to you for the tax year that started on 6 April 1997 and ended on 5 April 1998. The return also asks a few questions about the 1998-9 tax year to give the Revenue an idea of whether any major changes are expected in your circumstances.

Note

Our references to the tax return, supplementary pages, Inland Revenue guide and helpsheets are based on the drafts available when we went to press. The final versions of these documents may differ.

Which type of return do you need?

Everybody receives the standard eight-page tax return covering income from savings, investments, state benefits and pensions as well as allowances and reliefs. There are exceptions, for example partnerships and the partners working within them and trustees, for whom special tax returns have been produced.

In addition, you may also receive supplementary pages depending on what type of income you have. For example, if you are employed you will receive the supplementary page entitled 'Employment' (E1 and E2). If you are self-employed, you will receive 'Self-employment' (SE1 to SE4).

Page 2 of your tax return gives a list of all the supplementary pages. Read through this page and tick the boxes that apply to you. If you have new income during the tax year that your tax office doesn't know about (for example, if you start letting a property during the tax year), you won't receive the correct supplementary pages. It is your responsibility to ensure you have all the pages you need. You can order any supplementary forms (as well as any helpsheets) from the Inland Revenue orderline 0645 000 404.

Make sure your ticks correspond with the supplementary pages you fill in. Tackle the supplementary pages first and then turn to the standard eight pages of the tax return.

Getting it right first time

The Inland Revenue has to send some completed tax returns back to taxpayers because of errors or omissions. The Revenue will tell you if it finds any mistakes and may amend your return. If you disagree, query the amendment straight away. Here are some tips for avoiding common errors.

- **Not sure what to put?** Complete all boxes that apply to you. Don't put 'see accounts, statements, P60, etc.' List any queries in a covering letter. Better still, ring your tax office before sending back your return, quoting the reference on the return. For general enquiries, ring any tax enquiry centre. The Inland Revenue self-assessment helpline (0645 000 444) operates from 5pm to 10pm Monday to Friday and 8am to 10pm weekends. We give answers to common questions on page 16.

- **An employee?** Do read the Inland Revenue notes on employment that accompany the employment supplementary pages as there is a lot of useful detailed information. If you have more than one job, complete separate supplementary pages for each one.

- **An employee paying into a personal pension plan?** Put the gross premiums (page 5 of return), not the net figure you actually pay.

- **Company car?** Make sure you put the actual taxable benefit in box 1.16 on page E1 of the employment pages, not the car's list price.

- **Self-employed?** The self-employment pages are often not fully completed. Pay particular attention to the boxes after 3.70 to 3.75.

- **Round figures up and down** You can round down income details to the nearest pound, e.g. for £11.95 put £11. When you put outgoings, round up the figures in each section to the nearest pound, e.g. for £387.01 put £388. You can round up tax credits and tax deductions. If an entry in a particular box requires income and credits from several sources to

13

be added together, it is the aggregate figure that should be rounded.

- **Fixed interest investments** When you buy and sell certain stocks (including PIBs), part of the price may include a portion of the next interest payment. This is called 'accrued income'. You may have 'charges' or 'reliefs' for this type of income. The Inland Revenue tax return guide gives a detailed explanation of what to put where. See also leaflet *IR68 Accrued Income Scheme*.

- **Did you stop receiving interest from a particular source during tax year 1996-7 or 1997-8?** Read the notes called 'special cases' on page 9 of the Revenue tax return guide – you may have paid too much tax on interest payments which stopped during 1996-7. If interest stopped during tax year 1997-8 read this section for what to put on your tax return.

- **Do you have gains from a UK life policy?** If you put details in box 12.5 rather than 12.8, the Revenue will assume that no notional tax has been deducted from your gain before you received it and will tax you again. If you are not sure whether notional tax has been taken into account, ask your insurance company.

- **Do you have an exempt pension?** An exemption applies to some UK pensions awarded to former employees because of injury at work or a work-related illness. If this pension is more than you would have been given if you had retired at the same time on grounds of ordinary ill-health, the extra pension is exempt and need not be included in boxes 11.10 to 11.12. There is a 10 per cent deduction

14

from some pensions paid in respect of service to an overseas government. To qualify, these UK pensions must be paid by or through a public department, officer or agent of the overseas government.

- **Claiming allowances?** Read question 16 carefully. For example, don't claim both the married couple's allowance and the additional personal allowance.
- **Born before 6 April 1933?** Put your date of birth into box 21.4 to make sure you claim any higher age-related allowance.

Finally, *remember to sign and date your return.* Keep a note of the figures on your tax return or take a photocopy of the form before sending it back. Don't send your tax office a photocopy of your completed return. However, it will accept a photocopy provided you write your answers on the photocopy itself and sign it.

Computers

The Inland Revenue produces a free disk for personal computers, covering the standard eight-page tax return and the supplementary pages for employment. The disk will help you complete your return and do the calculations for you. For a copy, ring 0645 000 404. If you produce a return on a computer, make sure the Revenue has approved the design and wording, and check whether precise figures should be entered or whether the program can deal with rounded figures.

15

Common questions

Can I ignore tax-free income?

Yes. Don't include in the tax return:

- education grants and scholarships
- some damages for personal injury
- interest on tax rebates or on delayed compensation for injury or death
- statutory redundancy pay and some payments from employers
- housing benefit, council tax and rent rebates, home improvement grants
- adoption allowances and some social security benefits (see page 12 of the IR guide for a list)
- some maintenance (see page 76)
- income from family income benefit life insurance policies
- some insurance benefits received because you are sick, disabled or unemployed, including income from most permanent health insurance policies
- betting winnings and lottery prizes
- tax-free income from savings and investments.

What is my PAYE reference/what is my reference number?

The PAYE reference number is given to every employer. It is sometimes shown on your P60, always on P45 and PAYE coding notices. The format always starts with 3 numbers, i.e. 123/etc. The 10-digit reference number for tax returns is found on the front page of the tax return under 'Official Use' and on the Giro part of the payment slip with your statement of account.

What are the correct figures to put in box 1.8 (Payment from P60) and box 1.11 (Tax deducted)?

It's difficult to give a precise answer because most employers use a substitute form P60 and there is therefore no standard format. A useful rule of thumb is where there is only one employment, the P60 will have a figure under the headings 'Total for year' and also 'Pay in this employment'. The figures should be the same in both sets of boxes.

Where do I claim for mortgage payments paid under MIRAS?

There is nowhere on the tax return to claim MIRAS relief because you don't need to claim it. You make your interest payments net of relief and your lender claims the tax back direct from the Inland Revenue.

I've sold my house. Do I need to complete the capital gains pages?

Usually, no. It is normal for a capital gain on the disposal of your main residence to be covered by 'private residence relief', provided the property has not been previously let, or left vacant. If in doubt, see helpsheet *IR283 Private Residence Relief.*

Do I need to complete the share option pages?

This refers to shares acquired directly or indirectly through your employment. You can usually ignore these pages where the shares are acquired through an approved share option scheme. However, there are occasions where shares acquired under an approved scheme need to be declared. If in doubt, ask your tax office.

Where do I put details about my TESSA or PEP?

Put details at box 10.12 to 10.14 *only if* you closed the TESSA before the five-year period or you withdrew interest of more than £180 from cash held within your PEP. No other details need be given.

Do I need to send in dividend vouchers, P60s etc?

No. If your tax office requires more information, it will let you know.

Where do I put payments to my company pension scheme?

Usually, your pay as shown on your P60 takes into account any contributions to a company pension scheme. This is because full relief for payments to a company pension scheme are given by your employer through the payroll. So you don't normally have to include details of this type of pension.

Do I need to complete the trust pages to show the money I got from the estate of a deceased relative?

If the payment represents the final distribution from the estate, it is most likely a legacy and need not be shown on the tax return. However, any income you receive from a trust set up by the deceased may have to be shown. If in doubt, ask your tax office.

I am an employee. Can I claim any work-related expenses?

Possibly. Here's a list of common expenditure. Some you can claim; others you can't.

Yes Fees, books for full-time training courses in the UK lasting between four weeks and a year. Your employer must require or encourage you to go on the course, and pay you while you're on it. You

may be allowed the extra living and travel costs.
• Professional subscriptions relevant to job.

No Fees and books for other courses or evening classes. • Exam fees. • Resit courses or exams.

Yes Replacing, cleaning, repairing protective clothing and uniform necessary for your job, which you are required to buy. • Cleaning protective or functional clothing bought by your employer, if facilities are not provided.

No Ordinary clothes you could wear outside work.

Yes Maintaining and repairing factory/workshop tools and instruments you're required to provide.
• Replacing tools and instruments less any amount from sale of old ones, provided that the new ones are not inherently better than the old.

No Initial cost of instruments and tools – but you may be able to claim capital allowances.

Yes Reference books necessary for your job which you're required to provide. If the book's useful life is over two years, you may have to claim capital allowances instead. • Stationery that is used strictly for your job.

No Books useful, but not necessary, for your job.
• Stationery that is not used strictly for your job.

Yes Fees and subscriptions to professional bodies.
• Fees for keeping your name on a professional register approved by the Revenue if this is a condition of your employment.

Yes Expenses relating to entertaining customers if you can claim these expenses back from your employer or pay them out of an expense allowance specifically for entertaining.

19

No Any other entertaining expenses.

Yes Reasonable hotel expenses when travelling because of your job, if you have a permanent home.

No Travel to and from work.

Yes Use of home for work if it is an express or implied condition of your employment that you carry out some of your duties at or from home. ● You can normally claim a proportion of heating and lighting costs and possibly a proportion of telephone, cleaning and insurance costs.

Yes Interest on loans to buy equipment necessary for your job.

No Overdraft or credit card interest.

Yes Expenses incurred strictly in the course of doing your job, including the running costs of your own car within certain limits. ● You can claim the whole cost if you use your own car only and necessarily to do your job. ● You can claim a proportion of the cost if you use it privately as well. ● If your employer requires you to use your own car for business purposes, and you're paid less than it costs you, claim the extra cost up to the maximum allowed. ● If you pay for the running costs of a company car, claim a proportion of the cost for business mileage. ● Part or all of the interest on a loan to buy a car for business use.

CHECKING YOUR INCOME TAX

2

To get your taxable income:

- Add up all the income you receive in one tax year, including taxable benefits from your employer. Ignore any tax-free income and exclude payments not classed as income, such as any inheritance, gifts and capital gains. Subtract any allowable expenses. This sum is your gross income.
- Deduct any tax-allowable deductions (pension contributions, for example), to arrive at what's called your total income.
- Deduct your personal allowance and any other full relief allowances you may be entitled to (but not restricted allowances such as the married couple's allowance), and you will arrive at your taxable income.

Use this simple calculator to help check whether you've paid the right amount of income tax for the tax year ending on 5 April 1998. A tax calculation guide comes with your tax return and will allow you to work out your tax bill. But if you don't have to fill in a tax return, or if you do but your tax affairs are straightforward, you can use our calculator to get a quick idea of your income tax for 1997-8.

1997-8 income tax calculator

Make sure you enter the right figure in each box. See 'Using the calculator', p27, if you need more help.

1 ENTER YOUR INCOME AND ANY TAX ALREADY PAID OR DEDUCTED

Income from employment As well as your basic salary or wage, include commission, bonuses, tips, holiday pay, taxable income from a profit-sharing scheme, taxable sick and maternity pay, and the taxable value of fringe benefits (see p31). Deduct any contributions to your employer's pension scheme, charitable payments made through a payroll-giving scheme, any tax-free profit-related pay, and anything spent on allowable expenses that isn't reimbursed.

Taxable profits from self-employment and freelance earnings (after capital allowances and loss relief). Give figures for the accounting period ending in the 1997-98 tax year. Include tax paid through payments on account.

Pensions and social security benefits Enter only the taxable amount. For pensions from abroad, this is 90 per cent of the amount due.

Income from savings and investments Enter the amount of any taxable interest received from banks and building societies, National Savings accounts, etc. Also enter any dividend or distribution received from shares and unit trusts. Enter the amount received and any tax deducted, and add the two together to get gross income. Don't enter stock dividends or foreign income dividends from UK companies (enter these at row **B**, below).

Income from land or property If you let rooms under the rent-a-room scheme, don't enter any tax-free amount of rental income. Include tax paid through payments on account.

Other income For example, taxable maintenance or alimony and non-dividend income from trusts, settlements or the estates of people who have died.

Income with notional tax deducted 'Notional tax' counts as tax already paid, but cannot be reclaimed, even by non-taxpayers. Enter in row **B**

• **stock (also called 'scrip') dividends and foreign income dividends** Enter here:

• **taxable gains on UK life insurance** Only some insurance gains are taxable. Enter the taxable amount received in the 'Gross' box and 23 per cent of the gross figure in the 'Tax paid' box. This calculator will not work for you if you are a lower-rate taxpayer and receive life insurance gains.

NOW ADD UP ALL YOUR TAX PAID (EXCLUDING NOTIONAL TAX) AND GROSS INCOME. ENTER THE TOTALS IN THE BOXES, RIGHT

	Net	Tax paid	Gross
A			
B			

Tax already paid	Gross income

2 ENTER YOUR TAX-ALLOWABLE DEDUCTIONS

	Net	Tax relief already received	Gross

Pension contributions Enter payments to personal pension plans, retirement annuity contracts, free-standing AVCs and any life insurance bought through a personal pension plan. If you made payments net of tax relief, enter the tax relief in the 'Tax relief already received' box. Don't include any payments 'carried back' to a previous tax year.

Vocational training payments Enter amounts if you paid for your own qualifying training.

Charitable giving Enter gross amounts of any payments to charity, and the tax deducted, under a deed of covenant or the Gift Aid scheme (see p80). If you are a non- or lower-rate taxpayer, the Revenue may claw back the tax deducted.

Maintenance payments Enter payments here only if they were made under the old rules (see p74), they totalled more than £1,830 and they qualify for relief. Enter the amount above £1,830 (you enter the first £1,830 in step **9**).

Interest on qualifying loans Enter loan interest that qualifies for tax relief (eg to buy a house you rent out). Don't enter loan interest for buying your own home – you normally get relief on this at source through MIRAS. If you don't get relief through MIRAS, this calculator won't work for you.

NOW ADD UP ALL YOUR GROSS DEDUCTIONS AND TAX RELIEF ALREADY RECEIVED AND ENTER THE TOTALS IN THE BOXES, RIGHT.

Tax relief already received	Gross deductions

3 CALCULATE YOUR TOTAL INCOME AND TAX PAID

● **Deduct gross tax-allowable deductions from gross income to find your total income.** Enter the result at C and carry to step **4**.

Total income	**C**

Total tax paid	

● **Subtract tax relief already received from tax already paid.** Enter the result at **D** and carry to step **11**.

D	

4 DEDUCT YOUR FULL RELIEF ALLOWANCES

Enter your total income (**C** from step 3).

	C

Personal allowance If you were born after 5 April 1933, enter £4,045. If you were born on or before that date, you may get a higher allowance – see p79 for how to work this out.

	–

Blind person's allowance If you were entitled to this allowance, enter £1,280 here. If your spouse can claim the allowance but doesn't use it in full, enter any unused amount here and put in a claim to transfer it.

	–

DEDUCT ALLOWANCES FROM C TO FIND WHAT YOU WILL PAY TAX ON (YOUR TAXABLE INCOME).
If the result is a negative figure, enter zero.

	=	**E**

5 WORK OUT YOUR LOWER-RATE TAX BILL

Enter **E** (from step **4**). Multiply by 20% and enter the result at **F**.

$$E \times 0.20 = \boxed{} \quad \textbf{F}$$

IF E WAS £4,100 OR LESS, GO TO STEP 8. OTHERWISE, GO TO STEP 6 FIRST.

6 WORK OUT YOUR BASIC-RATE TAX BILL

Enter **E**.

$$\boxed{} \quad \textbf{E}$$

Add together figures **A** and **B** (from step **1**) and enter at **G**. This is your gross savings income.

$$- \quad \boxed{} \quad \textbf{G}$$

Deduct your gross savings income (**G**) from **E**. If the result is a negative figure, enter zero.

$$= \quad \boxed{} \quad \textbf{H}$$

Next, deduct the lower-rate tax band (£4,100). If the result is a negative figure, enter zero.

$$- \quad \boxed{4,100}$$

Multiply the result by 3% and enter at **I**.

$$= \quad \boxed{} \qquad \times 0.03 = \boxed{} \quad \textbf{I}$$

IF E WAS £26,100 OR LESS, GO TO STEP 8. OTHERWISE GO TO STEP 7 FIRST.

7 WORK OUT YOUR HIGHER-RATE TAX BILL

Enter **E**.

$$\boxed{} \quad \textbf{E}$$

Deduct the basic-rate tax limit of £26,100.

$$- \quad \boxed{26,100}$$

Multiply the result (**J**) by 17% and enter at **K**.

$$= \quad \boxed{} \qquad J \times 0.17 = \boxed{} \quad \textbf{K}$$

Enter in the left-hand box your gross savings income (**G**) or **J**, whichever is lower. Multiply by 3% and enter at **L**.

$$\boxed{} \qquad \times 0.03 = \boxed{} \quad \textbf{L}$$

8 ADD UP ALL THE TAX DUE (F + I + K + L). ENTER THE RESULT AT M

$$= \quad \boxed{} \quad \textbf{M}$$

9 DEDUCT EXTRA TAX RELIEF

Enterprise Investment Scheme/Venture Capital Trusts Enter amount paid which qualifies for tax relief and multiply by 20%.

Maintenance/alimony Enter first £1,830 of qualifying payments (see p73). Multiply by 15%.

[ ] x0.20 = [ ] –

[ ] x0.15 = [ ] –

Notional tax Enter any notional tax (the total of the two boxes in step **1**). Note that this calculator will not work for you if you did not need to complete step 6 and you received taxable life insurance gains.

[ ] –

Married couple's allowance, additional personal allowance and widow's bereavement allowance Enter amount you have claimed and multiply by 15% (see p66–7 and 69 for details of what you can claim).

[ ] x0.15 = [ ] –

NOW DEDUCT EXTRA TAX RELIEF FROM M (STEP 8). THIS IS YOUR TAX BILL. IF THE RESULT IS A NEGATIVE FIGURE, ENTER ZERO

= [ ] **N**

10 ADD CLASS 4 NATIONAL INSURANCE

Enter Class 4 National Insurance on taxable business profits. This is 6% of business profits between £7,010 and £24,180. If your profits are over £24,180, enter £1,030. Add to **N** and enter total at **O**.

+

= [ ] **O**

11 DEDUCT TAX ALREADY PAID

Enter the total tax paid figure (D) from Step **3** and deduct it from your tax liability (O) in Step **10**.

[ ] – **D**

THE RESULT IS YOUR TAX BILL OR, IF A MINUS FIGURE, YOUR TAX OVERPAID. (NOTE THAT YOU MAY NEED TO MAKE ADJUSTMENTS IF YOU HAVE ALREADY HAD A TAX REFUND DURING THE YEAR.)

= [ ] ❷

Who can use this calculator?

Most taxpayers will be able to use our simple calculator. However, it doesn't take account of:

- double taxation relief on income from abroad
- the fact that if you are an employee you get basic-rate tax relief on personal pension plans even if you are a non-taxpayer
- special rules if you have capital gains or receive taxable lump sums from life insurance or an employer
- life insurance top-slicing relief
- the rare cases where tax relief on mortgages is not given at source
- any over- or underpayments of tax from previous tax years
- when you have savings income and either you receive a taxable redundancy payment or life insurance gain, or your taxable income excluding savings (figure H) is within the lower-rate tax band (ie under £4,100), and you have taxable capital gains. In this case, the unused lower-rate band is used up against your capital gains before it is set against your dividends.

If these circumstances apply to you, you need one of the Inland Revenue's tax calculation guides. There are alternative versions if you have taxable capital gains or lump sums from life insurance or your employer. Call the Inland Revenue orderline on 0645 000 404 for a copy.

Using the calculator

- In the 'net' column put income after tax deducted at source (such as actual interest from a building society if paid after tax) and deductions treated as paid after basic-rate tax relief (such as covenant payments to charity). Taxable life insurance gains and some dividends have 'notional tax' deducted. This counts as tax paid, but can't be reclaimed, even by non-taxpayers. The calculator takes account of this.
- Put in the 'tax paid' or 'tax relief' column tax already paid on income, and tax relief already received on deductions. Include tax already paid through payments on account.
- Put in the 'gross' column your income before tax, and tax-allowable deductions before tax relief. The calculator first works out the tax due on your gross income minus gross tax-allowable deductions. It then takes into account any tax already paid and tax relief already received. So it's important to put the right figure. To find the gross amount, either add together your net amount plus the tax, or divide the net amount by 0.77 (0.8 for income from savings and investments).
- Don't include in the calculator any tax-free income.
- When you fill in the calculator, put outgoings and income in whole pounds – round down any pence on income, round up on outgoings. When you put the tax you've paid, however, include the exact amount (including pence).
- You and your spouse should use separate copies of the calculator. You should each put half of any joint

income and joint deductions unless you have already notified your tax office of a different split.

- Step 5 of the calculator works out 20 per cent tax on all your taxable income. Step 6 adds 3 per cent to that 20 per cent for the slice of income within the 23 per cent band. Step 7 adds another 17 per cent to the 23 per cent for income over the higher rate (40 per cent) threshold. The Inland Revenue uses this method in its self-assessment tax calculation guide.

- Only the personal allowance and blind person's allowance (step 4) give full tax relief. The married couple's, additional personal and widow's bereavement allowances (step 9) give restricted relief. For 1997-8, this is 15 per cent of £1,830 (£274.50) for each allowance, whatever your rate of tax. In the year of marriage, you may get less. If you're 65 or over you may get more. The married couple's allowance and blind person's allowance can be transferred between spouses. Include any transferred amount with your own allowances.

INCOME FROM A JOB OR PENSION

The keys to ensuring you pay the right tax are your payslip or pension notification and coding notice, if you get one.

Pay as you earn

Employers deduct tax from your pay or company pension through PAYE – Pay As You Earn. After the end of a tax year, your employer (or ex-employer in respect of pensions) will give you a P60 or equivalent form showing your pay for the tax year and the tax deducted. You will need it if you get a tax return to complete.

The Revenue gives employers a PAYE code for each employee or pensioner. It tells employers how much tax to deduct. Most codes consist of a letter and a number. The letter lets employers alter your code automatically each year in line with Budget changes. The number tells your employer how much tax-free pay you are allowed in each tax year.

The number is arrived at by adding up allowances and reliefs you are allowed and subtracting taxable benefits or income you get, such as a company car or state pension. The number produced by this sum is your tax-free income. Remove the last digit, insert the relevant code letter and you get your code. When added back, the last digit is assumed to be 9. So if your code is 404L, your tax-free pay is £4,049. You can earn one-twelfth of £4,049 free of tax each month, 1/52 each week.

You have a separate tax code for each job. Your allowances will be included in the code for your main job. So your pay from a second job will probably all be taxed at the basic rate or at 40 per cent if you are a higher-rate taxpayer. An adjustment will be made at the end of the tax year to remedy any under- or over-payment.

Changing jobs

Your employer should give you form P45 when you leave a job. It shows your PAYE code, pay for the tax year to date and tax deducted. Give it to your new employer so that the correct amount of tax can be deducted from your pay.

Without a P45, your new employer will operate the emergency code (see below) on a 'week one' or 'month one' basis, if this is your only or main job. This assumes each week or month is the first one of the tax year. No account is taken of any free-of-tax pay that may be due from the start of the tax year to the time you began working. You may pay too much tax for a while. Any overpayment will be refunded by your employer when your proper code comes through.

Stopping work

If you become unemployed during the tax year, you might not have used up all your tax-free pay. You may be entitled to a tax refund, although any jobseeker's

3

allowance or some of the income support that you receive can reduce the refund.

Your former employer should give you a P45; give this to the benefit office. If you are still not working at the end of the year, you will get a P60U. This shows the taxable benefits that you've received and the tax that you've paid. If you are not due to pay tax on benefits you get because your income for the year is too low, ask for form P50 to claim a refund. Inland Revenue leaflets *IR41* and *IR42* give more information.

Absences from work

Sick pay from your employer (including statutory sick pay) is normally taxable. Tax is collected through PAYE. If your sick pay is less than your tax-free pay, you will

receive a refund of tax already paid in addition to the sick pay.

State maternity allowance is tax-free but statutory maternity pay and employer's maternity pay are taxable. Tax is collected through the PAYE system.

Your first job
Your employer should give you form P46 to complete; send it to your tax office (although only if you earned £62 or more a week during 1997-8). Form P46 enables your employer to tell the Revenue about your job and to work out which PAYE code to use.

If this is your first regular job since full-time education and you haven't received jobseeker's allowance, or income support paid because of unemployment, you will be given an 'emergency' tax code – 404L for the 1997-8 tax year. This assumes your only allowance is the personal allowance. So you can earn one-twelfth of £4,049 free of tax – about £337 a month, £78 a week.

Tax won't be deducted until the tax-free pay you were entitled to in the months that you weren't working has been used up. So, if you are on code 404L and your first monthly pay day is in the fourth month of the tax year, you are entitled to earn £337.42 × 4 = £1,349.68 before tax starts to become due.

Your coding notice

Your coding notice shows how your PAYE code is worked out, but you won't necessarily get one automatically each year if your tax affairs are straightforward. The Revenue sends out most notices in January and February for the next tax year on 6 April. You may also be sent one if you query your code or if your circumstances change.

Allowances

Figures on the left-hand side of a notice give tax-free pay you're entitled to, such as the personal allowance. If you are 65 or over, you may see 'Estimated Income' – a guess of your annual income used for calculating age-related allowances. 'Guesstimates' of deductions qualifying for relief may also be shown based on, for example, what you paid last year.

Possible entries include:

- payments for allowable expenses incurred in your job, and professional subscriptions essential for your work
- payments to personal pension plans (or old-style retirement annuity contracts) and free-standing additional voluntary contribution schemes
- a loan or mortgage outside the MIRAS scheme that qualifies for tax relief
- maintenance payments you make that qualify for tax relief
- tax-allowable payments to charity.

With some deductions, such as personal pensions and charitable gifts, you will already have received basic-rate tax relief by paying less to start with. If so, there will be an entry only if you are entitled to higher-rate tax relief, and the amount shown will be adjusted to take account of this.

Restricted allowances

Married couple's allowance, widow's bereavement allowance, additional personal allowance, non-MIRAS mortgage interest and tax-allowable maintenance payments are all 'restricted allowances'. In 1997-8, relief was restricted to 15p for each £1 of allowance. A coding notice shows the full allowance on the left-hand side and an allowance restriction (or loan interest restriction for mortgage interest) on the right-hand side. To check the relief you've been given, deduct the restriction from the full allowance and multiply the result by your highest rate of tax.

Deductions

Entries in the right-hand column reduce your tax-free pay. They include:

- most fringe benefits from your job, such as private medical insurance
- other income from working not taxed under PAYE, such as part-time earnings, commission or tips
- taxable state pensions and benefits
- investment income received before tax, such as most taxable National Savings interest
- taxable rental income
- taxable maintenance payments received under a court order dated before 15 March 1988.

Tax owed from a previous year is shown as tax underpaid. This reduces your code sufficiently for you to pay extra tax equal to the amount you owe. If you pay tax at the higher rate (40 per cent), the additional tax you owe on investment income is collected by the entry next to higher rate adjustment.

New allowances or outgoings

You may become entitled to a new allowance or incur a new outgoing during the tax year. Tell your tax office and ask for a new code – otherwise, you may pay too much tax and need a refund at the end of the year. Also report any changes that reduce your code – for example, if you get tax relief through the PAYE system for personal pension plan contributions that you stop making.

What the code letters mean

L   You get the basic personal allowance.

H   As for L plus either additional personal or married couple's allowance and you are likely to pay basic-rate tax.

P   You get the full age-related personal allowance for someone aged 65 to 74.

V   You get the full age-related personal and married couple's allowance for a person aged 65 to 74 and you are likely to pay basic-rate tax.

T   Used in all other cases. The number in the code stands for your allowances. You might ask for this code if you don't want your employer to know your age or marital status.

K   You get this code if the deductions from your tax-free pay exceed your personal allowances. The excess over your allowances will be added to your income each pay period.

NT You pay no tax on this income.

BR You pay basic rate tax on all this income, and all
    your allowances have been given elsewhere.
    You're most likely to get this if it's a code for a sec-
    ond job.
DO You pay higher rate tax on all this income, and all
    your allowances have been allocated elsewhere.
OT You get no allowances. Tax is deducted at the
    lower, basic and then the higher rate, depending
    on your income.

National Insurance

Employees usually pay Class 1 National Insurance
unless they are above state pension age or earn less
than the lower earnings limit. This was £62 a week
(£3,224 a year) in 1997-8. If your pay was above the
limit, you paid 2 per cent on the first £62 a week in
1997-8, and 10 per cent on anything more up to the
upper earnings limit of £465 a week (£24,180 a year).

TAX ON YOUR FRINGE BENEFITS

If you work for an employer, you may get fringe benefits or 'benefits in kind'. Some are always taxable; the value of others depends upon your circumstances. If your earnings are low, or you are a director, different rules may apply.

The taxable value of most fringe benefits is the cost to your employer of providing them. If you are given something which belonged to your employer, you will generally pay tax on the market value when you receive it. Anything you pay towards the cost of a perk is deducted when working out the taxable value.

The taxable value of most fringe benefits appears on your coding notice and is deducted from your allowances, reducing your PAYE code. After the end of each tax year, your employer must give both you and the Revenue form P11D (or P9D). It shows the benefits you've received during the tax year and their taxable value. Put details on the employment supplementary pages of the tax return.

The £8,500 threshold

The taxable value of perks can depend on whether or not you earn at a rate of less than £8,500 a year, including the value of any benefits and expense payments (whether or not they are taxable). So if you earned a salary of £7,000 a year and had a perk (a car, say) with a taxable value of £2,000, you would exceed the limit. You would exceed the limit if you earned £4,500 for six months' work as this is equivalent to £9,000 a year. Several jobs with the same (or an associated) employer are treated as one job for deciding whether the £8,500 limit is reached.

Directors

Company directors always pay tax on benefits in kind unless all of the following apply:

- you (together with close family members and certain other associates) own or control a total of 5 per cent or less of the shares in the company
- you are a full-time working director, or work for a charity or non-profit-making company
- you are not also a director of an associated company
- you are below the £8,500 limit.

Tax-free benefits

You won't normally pay tax on:

- **employer's pension contributions** to an 'approved' or 'statutory' scheme
- **employer-paid and fees and subscriptions** paid to approved professional bodies
- **life and sick pay insurance** (if certain conditions are met), routine health checks and medical screening

- **the first 15p of luncheon vouchers** each working day
- **child care** provided by your employer on its premises, or where your employer is wholly or partly responsible for paying and managing the child care
- **free or subsidised canteen meals** provided for employees generally
- **necessary protective clothing** or a recognisable uniform required to be worn as part of your duties
- **small personal expenses**, such as laundry or calls home, paid for by your employer when you're away overnight on business, provided the amount is not more than £5 a night (£10 outside the UK)
- **specified removal and relocation expenses** when you have to move to a new job or are transferred and need to change your main residence, up to a maximum of £8,000 per move
- **genuinely personal gifts**, such as wedding gifts (but not money for a retirement gift); awards, but not money, for long service of 20 years or more (within limits)
- **gifts and goods from business contacts** costing up to £150, provided that the gift is not in recognition of particular services and has not been procured by your own employer
- **the value of any entertainment**, such as a business lunch, that is provided by someone other than your employer or your employer's associate companies (if any)
- **annual staff functions** (such as Christmas parties) that are open to all staff and cost £75 a head or less a year

- **prizes** of up to £5,000 in staff suggestion schemes
- **books and fees** paid for by your employer for some external training courses. Extra travel expenses and living costs may not be taxable either
- **redundancy counselling services**
- **in-house sports facilities** available to employees generally
- **retraining courses** for employees who are leaving, or who have left within the last year (within limits)
- **taxis home** paid for by employers if you occasionally work until 9pm or later. Public transport must have stopped or it would be unreasonable to expect you to use it
- **free parking** at or near work
- **essential travel, accommodation and subsistence** payments if you are temporarily absent from your normal workplace for up to 12 months (up to 24 months from 6 April 1998)
- **travel and subsistence payments** when public transport is disrupted or for severely disabled employees incapable of using public transport
- **cost of some legal claims against you** as an employee or the insurance to cover you paid by your employer (but not criminal fines, such as parking fines).

Sometimes taxable

The following benefits are taxable for directors and those earning £8,500 a year or more:

- **Loans of money** – there's no tax if the balance out-standing on cheap or interest-free loans is £5,000 or less. If loans are for more than this, you pay tax on the difference between the interest you pay on all your loans (including the first £5,000) and the 'official rate' – 7.25 per cent as we went to press. If the loan qualifies for tax relief (such as the interest on the first £30,000 of a mortgage on your main home) you get tax relief based on the official rate. There's no tax if your employer runs a lending business, and lends money to you on the same terms as the public. But any part of the loan that your employer waives is taxed as income.

- **Loans of things** – the taxable value of something your employer lends you is usually 20 per cent of the market value when the item was first lent to you or any other employee, *plus* annual expenses such as repairs, *less* anything you pay for it. If your employer gives you an item previously loaned (except a car), the taxable value is the higher of its market value when given less anything you pay for it and its market value when it was first loaned, less anything you pay towards it, less any amounts on which tax has already been paid.

- **Medical insurance** premiums paid by your employer.

- **Mobile phones** These have a taxable value of £200 unless you use them only for business or you pay your employer for the full cost of private use.

- **Company vans** For private use of a van, you pay tax on a flat amount of £500 a year. The amount is reduced if the van is four years old or more, or if it is shared.

41

Nearly always taxable

You usually have to pay tax on the following, whatever your income:

- **Low-rent and rent-free accommodation** The taxable value is usually the greater of the gross rateable value of the home or the rent paid by your employer, less any rent that you pay. If there is no rateable value, your employer must agree a gross value with the Inland Revenue. If your accommodation costs more than £75,000, you may have to pay an additional charge. But accommodation is tax-free if you have to live in the home to do your job properly (as a caretaker, say), or if living in the home enables you to do your job better and it is customary in your kind of employment, or if there is a special threat to your security and you live in your home as part of special security arrangements. (But note: there are special rules for directors).

- **Debts and credit cards** You are taxed on the amount of any debt, bill or liability settled or paid by your employer, but you can get tax relief for business expenses you've paid for with the card.

- **Travel and other vouchers** exchangeable for money, goods or services are always taxable.

- **Free and discounted goods** offered to employees are taxed on the extra cost to your employer of providing the perk to you, not on the normal cost of the goods or services.

Company cars

If you are below the £8,500 limit (see above) there's no tax on a company car. If you earn more than this limit you will have tax to pay.

Basic taxable value

The basic taxable value of your company car is 35 per cent of the car's list price at the time the car was first registered. You include VAT and car tax if paid (but not road tax), delivery charges, the list price of any accessory fitted before you get the car (including VAT, delivery and fitting), and any accessories, such as alloy wheels, that cost more than £100 (including VAT and delivery) fitted after you get the car. The increased price applies from the beginning of the tax year the accessory was fitted. Deduct anything you pay towards the purchase price of the car or its accessories up to a limit of £5,000.

Where there is no list price, the price has to be agreed with the Revenue. For 'classic cars' – those aged 15 years or more at the end of the year and with a market value of £15,000 or more (provided this is above the list price at registration) – the open market value on the last day of the tax year, or the last day you had the car, is used.

Anything an employer pays to convert a company car for use by a disabled person is excluded, provided certain conditions are met.

43

Reducing the taxable value

- Reduce the taxable value by one-third if you travel more than 2,500 business miles in the tax year, by two-thirds if you travel more than 18,000 business miles.
- Reduce the taxable value by one-third if the car is four or more years old at the end of the tax year.
- If you have the car for only part of the year, or if your normal car is not available for at least 30 consecutive days, reduce the taxable value in line with the proportion of the tax year the car was unavailable.
- Deduct anything you pay your employer for private use of the car.

If you qualify for more than one reduction, you apply each in turn. So if you travel 20,000 business miles a year and your car is five years old, first reduce the taxable value by two-thirds and then reduce this new figure by a third. Anything you pay for private use of the car should be deducted last.

What your employer pays for business fuel, repairs, insurance and so on does not affect the taxable value. If you pay these costs yourself and you're not reimbursed, claim the amounts relating to your job on your tax return.

Two cars

If you have two or more cars in succession in a tax year, the 2,500-mile and 18,000-mile thresholds apply to each car separately, reduced in proportion to the number of days you had each car during the year. A second company car provided for you or a member of your family is taxed like the first car, but there is no reduction for business mileage between 2,500 and 17,999 miles. If business use is 18,000 miles or more, you get only a one-third reduction.

Fuel charges

You are taxed if your employer buys any fuel for your private use. Journeys between home and work count as private use. The taxable value is based on engine size, not on the amount of fuel provided. 1997-8 taxable values were £800 (£740 for diesel) up to 1,400cc, £1,010 (£740 for diesel) between 1,401cc and 2,000cc, £1,490 (£940 diesel) over 2000cc.

Pool cars

There's no tax to pay if you use a pool car – one available to, and used by, more than one employee. It shouldn't normally be kept overnight at or near an employee's home. Private use of the car must be merely incidental to business use.

Your own car

If you use your own car for work, your employer usually reimburses your expenses. Most employers pay a set amount per mile; some also pay a regular fixed sum (every month, say). These payments are usually made without tax being deducted but they are taxable. You can, however, claim tax relief up to certain limits. There are two main ways:

- **Fixed Profit Car Scheme** Some employers agree a profit table, based on engine size and mileage, with

45

the Inland Revenue under the Fixed Profit Car Scheme (FPCS). This provides an estimate of the taxable profit on mileage allowances paid by that employer. As the table includes some averages or estimates, you may be better off using the Revenue's published rates.

- **Inland Revenue 'authorised mileage' rates** (previously called FPCS rates). Use these rates for tax purposes if your employer doesn't run a FPCS or if you want to work out your own mileage profit. To do this, multiply the Revenue's rate for your engine size by the number of business miles you did during the tax year. Compare the result with the amount you received from your employer (including any regular sum). You pay tax on any excess.

Authorised mileage rates 1997-8 and 1998-9

Engine size of car used (cc)	Relief per business mile up to 4,000 (p)	Relief per business mile over 4,000 (p)
up to 1000	28	17
1001 to 1500	35	20
1501 to 2000	45	25
over 2000	63	36

WORKING FOR YOURSELF

Self-employed people and those working in partnerships enjoy more favourable tax treatment than employees. They have greater scope to deduct business expenses from income and pay lower National Insurance contributions (but get reduced rights to state benefits). If your business is run as a limited company, the rules are different from those below. For details, contact your tax office.

Taxes you may pay

Income tax
You will have to pay income tax if your profits from self-employment plus other income come to more than your tax-allowable outgoings and allowances. Individual partners are treated as sole traders and are taxed on their share of the partnership profits.

National Insurance 1997-8
You pay Class 2 contributions at a flat rate of £6.15 a week. You can elect not to pay if your profits are less than £3,480, but this affects your entitlement to certain state benefits such as retirement pension. You also pay Class 4 contributions, 6 per cent on taxable profits between £7,010 and £24,180 – a maximum payment of just over £1,030. You pay nothing on up to £7,010.

Your contributions are capped if you work for an employer and for yourself – see DSS leaflet *CA72*.

You pay employer's National Insurance contributions (secondary Class 1) if you employ someone earning more than £62 a week.

Value added tax (VAT)

From 1 December 1997, you have to register for VAT if, at the end of any month, the taxable turnover of all your business activities in the year ending on the last day of that month exceeds £49,000 (*from 1 April 1998 the threshold increases to £50,000*). At or below this limit you decide whether to register.

Registration can cut your expenses (you can reclaim VAT on things you buy for business) but you have to add VAT to the price you charge your customers (not a problem if your customers are also VAT-registered businesses). Contact your local VAT office (see 'Customs and Excise' in the phone book) for more details.

Business rates

You pay business rates if you have business premises, such as a shop or offices, or if part of your home is used exclusively for business. If it is used for both business and domestic purposes, business rates should not be levied and you may be able to claim part of your council tax as an allowable business expense.

Are you self-employed?

You must be genuinely working for yourself. Can you answer 'yes' to the following questions?

- Do you have the final say about how your business is run (for example, do you decide where you work and the hours that you work)?
- Do you put your own money at risk?
- Do you bear any losses, as well as keep the profits?
- Do you provide the major equipment needed for your work (office equipment, a car, a van or specialist machinery, for example)?
- Are you free to hire people on terms you choose to do work that you have taken on? Do you pay them out of your own pocket?
- Do you have to correct unsatisfactory work in your own time and at your own expense?

If you answered 'no' to some of the questions, get a copy of the joint Inland Revenue and Department of Social Security leaflet *IR56/NI39*. You can ask your tax office for a decision in writing on whether you count as self-employed. If the conditions of your contracts vary from job to job, your employment status could also vary from job to job.

Starting up

In your first year you are taxed on your actual profits from the date your business started up to the end of the tax year in April. This is a proportion of the profits in your first accounting period. Say you started up on 6 January 1998, your first accounting period ends on 31 December 1998, and your profit for this period is £10,000. Your assumed profit in the three months to 5

April 1998 (i.e. for the 1997-8 tax year) will be 3/12 x £10,000 = £2,500.

In their second tax year, most businesses are taxed on the profits for the 12 months up to the accounting date in that year. If you are making up your first accounts and they cover less than a year, you are taxed on your profits for the first 12 months of trading. Where there is no accounting date in the second tax year, you are taxed on your profits for the tax year itself.

In the third and subsequent years, tax is based on profits for the accounting year ending during the new tax year.

Overlap profits

Under the opening year rules (and in the transition to self-assessment for existing businesses) some profits may be taxed more than once. They are called 'overlap profits' and you get 'overlap relief' when you eventually close your business, or sooner if you change your accounting date to later in the tax year.

Ideally, you want as little overlap profit as possible because inflation erodes the value of the relief. You have no overlap profit (and avoid the complications of opening year rules) if you choose 'fiscal accounting'. This means having an accounting year coinciding with the tax year (an end-March accounting date will qualify). The drawbacks are that you pay tax earlier and you have less time to draw up your accounts than if you choose an accounting date earlier in the year.

Closing down

If you closed down during 1997-8, you will be taxed in that tax year on your profits from your last accounting date up to the date of closure, less any overlap profit carried forward. If your business started *before* 6 April 1994, special rules may apply to the two previous years: generally, 1995-6 will have been taxed on the old previous-year basis and 1996-7 on the transitional basis. Your tax office can choose, instead, to tax you on your actual profits for 1995-6 and 1996-7, if this would produce a higher tax bill – see Inland Revenue leaflet *IR105*.

What you pay tax on

Taxable profits are, broadly, your yearly takings less business expenses but with various adjustments.

Stock values
You can deduct the cost of raw materials or goods bought for resale if they are actually sold during the year. The value put on stocks is generally their cost to you or their market value if lower. Market value is the replacement price if you are a merchant, the retail price if you are a retailer.

Money owed
Accounts normally have to be kept on an 'accruals' basis. This means that you include income in your accounts when you sell goods or do work and expenses when they are due, regardless of whether you have received or made any payment. Some peo-

ple following a vocation (but not a trade) can opt for a 'cash' basis subject to certain conditions and the Inland Revenue's agreement.

Capital allowances

When you buy capital equipment (items not for resale and of lasting use to the business, such as computers or cars), you do not deduct their cost from profits but must claim 'capital allowances' instead. The cost of each capital item is added to a 'pool of expenditure'. When calculating taxable profits, you can usually deduct up to 25 per cent from the pool as a 'writing-down' allowance. But for capital items bought between 2 July 1997 and 1 July 1998 inclusive, you might be able to claim a first-year capital allowance of 50 per cent (instead of the normal 25 per cent writing-down allowance). You will qualify for this concession if two out of the following three conditions apply: your turnover is no more than £11.2 million a year, your assets are valued at no more than £5.6 million; you have 250 or fewer employees.

If you sell a capital item, the sale proceeds are deducted from the pool before the writing-down allowance is worked out. If the proceeds of all the items you sell come to more than the value of the pool, the excess (which is called a 'balancing charge') is added to your profits for the year and taxed.

If you sell an item for less than its written-down value, you will normally have to claim tax relief on the residue when the business ceases, unless you elected to have it treated as a 'short-life asset'. Capital items with an expected life of less than five years – computers, say – can be treated as 'short-life assets'. If you stop using them within five years, you get immediate tax relief when you dispose of them. These must be put in a separate pool.

Keep separate pools for cars (not lorries or vans) and for assets used both privately and for business – you get a proportion of the allowances equal to the business use. A car costing £12,000 or more must be recorded in its own individual pool, and there is a £3,000 maximum yearly allowance.

Using your losses

Losses can reduce your overall tax liability now or in the future, or even in the past in certain circumstances. A loss incurred in an accounting year can be:

- carried forward indefinitely to set against profits from the same business in future years
- set against any other income in the new tax year – if this does not use up the whole loss, you can set the remainder against any capital gains for the year
- set against any other income for the previous tax year, provided the business was carried on in that year – if this does not use up the whole loss, you can set the remainder against any capital gains for that year
- set against your income (but not capital gains) from the previous three tax years if the loss is incurred in the first four tax years of your business
- set against profits from the business over the previous three years if the loss is incurred in the last 12 months before closing down.

53

Allowable expenses

Broadly speaking, you can deduct from your business income any costs that you incur in running your business, provided they are incurred 'wholly and exclusively' for the purpose of the business. You can usually claim a proportion of payments made partly for business and partly for personal reasons, such as the cost of running a car used partly for business and some domestic bills if you work from home. If you are registered for VAT, deduct VAT from the cost of any expenses you claim. Below we list expenses which are normally allowed and those not normally allowed. The list is not exhaustive.

Cost of sales

Yes The cost of goods for resale and the cost of raw materials; discounts on sales; payments to subcontractors and the cost of materials supplied in the construction industry; fuel costs if you are a taxi driver, road haulage contractor, etc; cost of small tools.

No Fuel for private use if you are a taxi driver, road haulage contractor, etc.

Employee costs

Yes Recruitment agency fees; wages, salaries and redundancy payments to employees; insurance costs and pension benefits for employees and their dependants; training costs; the cost of temporary secondment of your employees to certain charitable and educational organisations; some types of child care provision for the children of your employees; employer's National Insurance contributions for employees; the cost of hiring locums or subcontractors; insurance premiums to cover providing locums in the event of your being ill; 'keyman' insurance for employees; staff entertainment such as the Christmas party (but only up to certain limits).

No Your own wages, salary or drawings from the business, or those of your business partners; wages paid to family members if these are excessive for the work done; the cost of premises and equipment for a workplace crèche (although this may qualify for capital allowances); your own National Insurance contributions and income tax; your own pension costs (although you can get personal tax relief on these); your own life, 'keyman', accident, permanent health and private medical insurance.

Premises costs

Yes Heating; lighting; cleaning; water rates; rent for business premises; business rates; council tax on a second home used for business. If you work from home: a proportion of the lighting, heating, cleaning and insurance costs; a proportion of rent (and domestic rates in Northern Ireland) or of mortgage interest if part of your home is used exclusively for business (although be aware that there may then be a capital gains tax bill when you sell your home; probably a proportion of council tax, although this might affect your capital gains tax position.

No The initial cost of buildings (but this may qualify for a capital allowance); council tax relating to the private use of your main home.

Repairs

Yes General maintenance of business premises (a proportion if you work from home); repairs to and replacement of business equipment.

No Alterations and improvements to business premises (although these may qualify for capital allowances).

General admin

Yes Phone bills (a proportion only if you also use the phone for private purposes); postage; stationery; printing; delivery costs; computer software with limited lifetime; relevant books and magazines.

No Most payments to clubs, charities, etc; money paid as a result of extortion.

Motor expenses

Yes The running costs of your own car, such as insurance, servicing, repairs, road tax and petrol (a proportion only if it is also used privately); the cost of hiring cars or vans; parking charges.

No Travel between your home and your workplace; the cost of buying a vehicle (although this may qualify for capital allowances); parking and motoring fines.

Travel and subsistence

Yes Travel and accommodation on business trips; travel between different places of work; travel to

and from the UK exclusively for business reasons
to carry out business performed wholly outside
the UK.

No   Meals, except a reasonable amount for breakfast
and evening meal on overnight trips.

Publicity and entertainment

Yes   Newspaper and magazine advertisements, mail-
shots and other forms of promotion; free samples;
gifts up to £10 a year to any one person provided
that they advertise your business and the gifts are
not food, drink, tobacco or vouchers for goods.

No   Business entertainment such as lunches with
clients; most gifts.

57

Legal and professional costs

Yes   Accountants' fees; solicitors' fees; some costs of architects and surveyors; the cost of your professional indemnity insurance.

No   The cost of settling tax disputes; legal fees and fines due to breaking the law; the cost of buying premises and equipment (although this may qualify as a capital allowance).

Bad debts

Yes   Money owed to you and unlikely to be paid.

No   General reserves for bad debts.

Borrowing and finance

Yes   Interest on bank loans and other forms of credit. Bank charges, credit card charges and the interest element of hire purchase charges; leasing costs.

No   Capital repayments; the capital element of hire purchase charges.

Other expenses

Yes   Special clothing for work; fees paid to register trade marks and designs.

No   The cost of clothes you could wear for non-work purposes; the cost of buying a patent from someone else (although this qualifies as a capital allowance).

AT HOME WITH TAX

You can get tax relief on interest paid on up to £30,000-worth of loans used to buy your main home (or part share of it) in the UK or Republic of Ireland. In 1997-8 relief was 15 per cent of the interest. From 6 April 1998 it falls to 10 per cent.

The £30,000 applies to each property. Before August 1988 it applied to individual borrowers. Unmarried joint borrowers each claimed tax relief up to £30,000. If you have a joint mortgage taken out before August 1988, you will lose any relief you may have on loans above £30,000 if you remortgage with another lender or marry another joint borrower.

Most home purchase loans are covered by the Mortgage Interest Relief at Source (MIRAS) scheme. Your lender deducts tax relief from what you have to pay and claims it direct from the government. If your loan isn't in MIRAS, you pay the interest in full and get tax relief through an adjustment to your PAYE coding or by a reduction in your final tax bill. Claim the relief on your tax return. Get a certificate of interest paid from your lender, in case the Revenue asks to see it.

Special MIRAS rules

- If you move home, you can get tax relief on your old home for up to a year, even if you aren't living there, so long as you are actively trying to sell it. This won't affect the tax relief on your new home.

- You can live away from home for up to a year at a time before you stop receiving mortgage interest relief. And if your employer requires you to live away from home, you can get tax relief for up to four years, provided you are likely to use it as your only or main home when you return. Crown Servants and members of the armed forces working abroad get relief until the end of their overseas posting.

- If you let your home while you are away, the loan must usually be taken out of MIRAS. The Revenue may let you keep it in MIRAS if you can prove that you intend to use the property again as your main residence when you come home. But there can be advantages in getting out of MIRAS – see page xx.

- If you live in a home that goes with your job and counts as a tax-free fringe benefit, you may be enti- tled to interest relief on a property that you use as an occasional residence, or that you intend to use as your only or main home in due course.

- Arrears of up to £1,000 added to your loan still qual- ify for tax relief provided the total loan was less than £30,000 before the arrears were added.

- Non-taxpayers get relief automatically if the loan is in MIRAS. If it isn't, ask your tax office for how to get tax relief. If you don't have a tax office, write to Financial Intermediaries and Claims Office, Advice on Schemes (MIRAS), St John's House, Merton Road, Bootle L69 9BB, with details of your mortgage.

Letting your property

If you start letting your property part-way through a tax year, you must tell the Inland Revenue. It will probably ask you to fill in a tax return. Most rental income is taxed under the rules of 'schedule A' and treated as investment income rather than trading income or income from employment. The rules apply to rents from property, chargeable premiums on leases, ground rents and feu duties (as ground rents are known in Scotland).

Ordinary rental income

If your income is treated as schedule A rental income, you are taxed on an 'earnings' basis. This means your 1997-8 tax bill is based on rent earned from the tenants' use of the property between 6 April 1997 and 5 April 1998, less your allowable expenses. Suppose, for example, that you are paid rent twice a year, in advance, on 2 January and 1 July. A proportion of the payment made on 2 January 1997 would be taxable in the 1996-7 tax year (the amount due between 2 January and 5 April 1997); the rest of the rent would be taxed in the 1997-8 tax year. Calculate the rent on a daily basis and multiply by the number of days in the tax year.

You have to declare rental income that is due in the tax year, even if you are not paid until after the tax year is over. However, you can deduct rent not received from your total rental income if you have tried but failed to collect the rent and, sometimes, if you have waived rent to avoid hardship to the tenant.

Rent-a-room scheme

Both owner-occupiers and tenants can claim rent-a-room relief if they let part of their only or main home as furnished accommodation. You pay no tax at all on gross rents (i.e. including charges for meals, cleaning, laundry and so on) of up to £4,250 in the 1997-8 tax year. You are taxed on anything over £4,250 and get no tax relief on any expenses. If your expenses exceed £4,250, it may be better to be taxed under schedule A instead. Where more than one person receives rent on one property, the exemption limit is £2,125 per person.

To claim rent-a-room relief, answer 'yes' to the relevant question on the land and property supplementary of the tax return. Tell your mortgage lender and insurers if you let rooms in your home. Otherwise, you could breach the contractual agreements you have with both.

Rents as trading business income

Income from letting rooms in your home may count as business trading income if you live in the property and provide services beyond those normally offered by a landlord, for example if you run a bed and breakfast or a guest house. Put such income on the self-employment supplementary pages of the tax return.

The main advantages of trading income over ordinary schedule A rental income are:

- you can use trading income to pay personal pension premiums
- you can claim capital allowances on items such as furniture and furnishings
- capital gains tax rollover and retirement reliefs are available
- trading income losses can be offset against other income for the year, whereas schedule A rental losses can be offset only against rental income.

Holiday lettings

Your home, caravan or mobile home is treated as holiday accommodation if available for letting to the general public on a commercial basis for at least 140 days during each 12-month period. It must actually be let for 70 of these days, and during at least seven of the 12 months no tenant may occupy it for more than 31 days in one stretch.

Income from furnished holiday accommodation may be considered as trading income (see above)

although you put details on the land and property supplementary pages of the tax return. Check with your tax
office if you're not sure.

Allowable expenses

When working out your profits, subtract from rental
income expenses wholly and exclusively incurred rent-
ing out your property. If you let only part of your home,
or let it for only part of each year, you have to agree
with the Revenue the proportion of these expenses you
can claim. The most common allowable expenses are:

- water rates, ground rents and council tax
- normal repairs and decoration, but not improvements or additions
- wear and tear, including wear and tear of furnishings
  such as cookers and carpets if the property is fully
  furnished: you can claim *either* on a renewals basis,
  claiming the cost of any items replaced during the
  year (excluding improvements), *or* a set 10 per cent
  of the rent after deducting council tax, water rates
  and other services you pay which would usually be
  paid by a tenant – you must stick to the same
  method every tax year
- management expenses, such as phone bills,
  accountant's fees and cost of rent collection
- insurance valuations and premiums
- legal fees for renewing a tenancy agreement
- estate agent's or accommodation agency's fees and
  the cost of advertising for tenants
- the cost of services you provide, including the wages
  of people such as cleaners and gardeners

- bills such as gas and electricity
- the cost of preparing an inventory
- mortgage interest, as long as you don't claim MIRAS (see below).

Mortgage interest

You can claim tax relief on all mortgage interest at your top rate of tax. However, you can deduct the interest only from rental income. Interest counts as an expense so losses in one year can be carried forward and offset against future rental income.

If you are eligible for both MIRAS relief and relief under the rules for letting, choose the most advantageous one. Generally, tax relief under the rules for letting is best unless you have too little income to set against the interest or you're a non-taxpayer and can't get tax relief on your mortgage any other way.

Services

If you charge separately for services like cleaning or laundry, the income you receive is not treated as rent unless you are in the rent-a-room scheme. It is assessed separately. Put details on the land and property supplementary pages of the tax return. Expenses from providing these services can be subtracted from the income.

Losses

If you make a loss in one tax year, you can carry this forward to be set against rental income in future years. You may have losses under the old rules (before 5 April 1995) that haven't been used in this way. If so, they can normally be offset against rent received during 1995-6.

You and Your Family

Whether you're living with a partner, married, widowed, separated or divorced, there are tax rules that may affect you.

Tax and marriage

Husband and wife each receive a basic personal allowance of £4,045 for the 1997-8 tax year (possibly more if you are over 64 – see page 79). In addition, married couples can claim the married couple's allowance of £1,830. It's worth 15 per cent of £1,830 - £274.50. This is subtracted from your tax bill.

- You lose one-twelfth of the 1997-8 allowance if you married after 6 May, two-twelfths if you married after 6 June, and so on. Tell your tax office the date of your wedding, so that your allowances (and PAYE code, if relevant) can be adjusted.
- The allowance automatically goes to the husband unless husband and wife elect jointly for the whole allowance to go to the wife *or* one spouse unilaterally elects to receive half of it.
- To reallocate the married couple's allowance, ask your tax office for form 18. Tick the relevant box on your tax return (if you get one). Apply before the start of a tax year on 6 April to get the allowance reallocated for the coming tax year.

- If the tax you pay over a year ends up being less than the value of your allowance, you can also transfer the unused part to the other spouse retrospectively. You must do this within five years of the end of January after the relevant tax year (by 31 January 2004 for the 1997-8 tax year).

Special transitional rules were introduced in April 1990 to make sure a married couple's combined allowances did not reduce when husbands and wives started to be taxed independently. Few people are now affected by these rules.

Married couples can transfer the blind person's allowance if the recipient cannot make full use of it.

If your spouse dies

You may be able to claim the following allowances:

- widow's bereavement allowance, worth up to £274.50 (15 per cent of £1,830) in 1997-8 (women only)
- widow's bereavement allowance for the tax year following your husband's death, if you haven't remarried (women only)
- married couple's allowance: if your husband didn't have sufficient income to use it all – the married couple's allowance is given wholly to the husband in the year of his death regardless of any election you made (women); if some or all of the allowance was allocated to the wife, you use any part unused by the wife (men)

67

- additional personal allowance (see below) if a dependent child lives with you (men and women).

Joint investment income

If you and your spouse have investments in joint names, you normally each pay tax on half the investment income. If you own the investments in unequal shares, the income can be taxed the same way if you complete form 17 (from your tax office). If husband and wife have different top rates of tax, it makes sense to transfer income-paying investments to the person paying the lower rate. The transfer of ownership must be genuine.

Your home

If you get married and you buy a new home together, you can continue to get tax relief on loans on your old homes (for up to 12 months) provided they are up for sale. This is in addition to tax relief on up to £30,000 of loans on a new home you buy. If one of you moves into the other one's home, you can continue to receive tax relief for up to 12 months on the home that you decide to sell.

Who gets the tax relief?

Mortgage tax relief is usually split evenly between a married couple if they have a joint mortgage, or given to the sole borrower if it isn't joint. However, you can elect to split the interest for tax purposes, even if one of you pays it all, by completing form 15 (ask your tax office for it). It is worth doing this only if one spouse pays very little (or no) tax, and you don't receive relief under MIRAS.

Additional personal allowance

A separated, widow(er)ed or unmarried parent who lives with a dependent child can claim the additional personal allowance of £1,830. Like the married couple's allowance, this is worth up to £274.50 (15 per cent of the £1,830). Two single parents living as a couple can have only one additional personal allowance between them. A man with a dependent child receiving the additional personal allowance can opt to keep it for the tax year of marriage instead of claiming the married couple's allowance. This is worth doing if he marries after 6 May.

A married man living with a wife who is totally incapacitated through illness or injury for all or part of the year, and who has a child living with him, can claim the additional personal allowance as well as the married couple's allowance.

Children

Children have the same personal allowance as adults. However, income given to a child by a parent (or income from an asset given by a parent) counts as the parent's income unless it is no more than £100 a year from each parent. If the income exceeds £100, the whole lot is taxed as the parent's.

69

Income accumulating in a 'bare' trust is also treated as the child's, even if from a parent. No income can be withdrawn before the child reaches age 18, and you cannot stop your child taking over the trust assets at that age.

SPLITTING UP AND MAINTENANCE

8

Unmarried couples

If you have more than one child and at least one lives with each parent, each parent can claim the additional personal allowance from the tax year following the year in which you part.

Married couples

In the tax year married couples part, each gets the proportion of married couple's allowance they were receiving when they separated. A spouse who lives with a child but receives no married couple's allowance can claim the additional personal allowance. If each spouse was receiving half the married couple's allowance, and they have two or more children who live with each of them for part of the year, each can claim half (i.e. £915) of the additional personal allowance. If there is only one child, who lives with each parent for part of the year, the couple can claim only £915 between them.

A married couple getting back together in the same tax year as they split up are taxed as if there had been no separation. If they get back together in a later tax year, they will get the full married couple's allowance in the year of reconciliation, as long as a decree absolute has not been issued.

Subsequent years

You are each taxed as single people in tax years after you separate. If your children spend time living with both of you, the additional personal allowance can be split (see Inland Revenue leaflets *IR92* and *IR93* for more details).

If you split up before 6 April 1990 and you wholly maintain your separated wife with voluntary payments, you can continue to claim the married couple's allowance until the decree absolute. If this applies to you and you can claim the additional personal allowance, or if you are divorced, you may be better off making enforceable maintenance payments and claiming the maintenance deduction (see below).

Your home

From the date you split up, you are each entitled to tax relief on interest on loans of up to £30,000 for a new home, provided you each pay your own interest. If one of you stays in the old home you can buy out the share of the person who is leaving and carry on getting relief of up to £30,000. If you pay your ex-spouse's mortgage and the loan was taken out after 5 April 1988, there is no tax relief on the interest. It is usually better to pay extra maintenance, so your ex-spouse can pay his or her mortgage direct. You get tax relief on a mortgage of your own.

Capital gains tax

There is normally no capital gains tax to pay on gifts between spouses. However, this doesn't apply if you're divorced or if you're separated (except in the tax year of separation) or to unmarried partners.

Inheritance tax

Gifts between husband and wife are exempt from inheritance tax unless the recipient's domicile (broadly, their permanent home) is outside the UK, when there is a £55,000 limit on gifts. This exemption is lost on divorce but there is still no inheritance tax to pay on:

- money paid as part of the divorce settlement
- maintenance payments to a former partner or children, including adopted and stepchildren, who are under 18 or in full-time education
- in some cases, money given to you following a change to an agreement you made on or before your divorce.

Paying maintenance

To get tax relief on maintenance payments they must be enforceable – i.e. made under an assessment from the Child Support Agency, a court order or a legally binding agreement, including those made in other European Union countries (since 6 April 1992) and the European Economic Area (since 1 January 1994). Payments under court orders or agreements made outside the EEA rarely qualify for tax relief. Voluntary maintenance doesn't qualify for tax relief.

Enforceable maintenance arrangements set up since 15 March 1988 are taxed under the 'new' rules. Those set up before that date may still be taxed under the 'old' rules.

The new rules

If you make enforceable maintenance payments, you can claim the 'maintenance deduction' unless your ex-spouse remarries. You get tax relief of 15 per cent of payments up to a limit of £1,830 in the 1997-8 tax year, reducing your tax bill by up to £274.50. Maintenance must be paid directly to your ex-spouse for his/her maintenance or that of a child aged under 21. And it is not available if the order says that payments are to be made directly to your children.

You cannot claim the maintenance deduction for lump sums paid as part of the divorce settlement (even if they are paid in instalments), or for payments for which you already receive tax relief – mortgage payments, for example.

The old rules

In 1997-8, tax relief on the first £1,830 you pay is limited to 15 per cent. On payments above £1,830, you will get relief at your highest rate of tax. However, relief is limited to the amount of maintenance on which you had relief in the 1988-9 tax year.

So if you paid £2,000 to your ex-spouse in 1988-9, you will get tax relief only up to a maximum of £2,000, even if you now pay more. You'll get 15 per cent relief on the first £1,830, and relief at your highest rate of tax on the balance of £170.

The old rules give tax relief on maintenance you pay under a court order to children, subject to a limit of the amount you paid in the 1988-89 tax year. Relief on the first £1,830 (for 1997-8) is restricted to 15 per cent, and on the rest you will get relief at your highest rate of tax. The maintenance payment to the child will be counted as the child's own income and is therefore taxable. The child may use his or her own personal allowance to reduce the tax. If the payments are made to the custodial parent then, under the old rules, the maintenance payment will be taxable as the parent's income.

New or old rules?

Under the new rules, relief is available only on payments up to a limit of £1,830 (in the 1997-8 tax year). If your payments are greater than this, and you are taxed under the old rules, you should stick with this system.

If your maintenance is taxed under the old system, your payments are less than £1,830, and your former spouse has not remarried and is unlikely to remarry in the future, you may be better off switching to the new system if your maintenance payments have increased. However, if you make maintenance payments directly to children, you will lose all the tax relief on these payments.

You can elect to switch to the new rules at any time during the tax year for which your election is to apply, or within 12 months of the end of the January after the relevant tax year (by 31 January 2000 for the 1997-8 tax year). Get form 142 from your tax office. You also have to inform the recipient in writing. Once you've switched to the new rules, you can't change back.

Receiving maintenance

Enforceable maintenance arrangements set up since 15 March 1988 are taxed under the 'new' rules. Those set up before that date may still be taxed under the 'old' rules.

The new rules
Maintenance payments are treated as tax-free income regardless of whether you're getting them from an ex-spouse, ex-partner, parent or step-parent.

The old rules
Voluntary payments are not taxable. If you receive enforceable maintenance from an ex-spouse, the first £1,830 is tax-free, unless you remarry, in which case it becomes taxable. Anything above this amount counts as taxable income. But the taxable amount is limited to the amount on which you were liable to pay tax in the 1988-9 tax year. Increases since 5 April 1989 are tax-free.

Again, with the exception of increases since 5 April 1989, enforceable maintenance from a parent or step-parent to a child under 21 and paid under a court order or legally binding agreement is taxable. The tax will be collected either through self-assessment, or by adjusting the child's PAYE coding.

If the person who pays you maintenance changes to the new rules, none of the maintenance that you get will be taxed.

TAX FOR OLDER PEOPLE

Most pensions are taxable, but some are paid without tax deducted at source.

Pensions from the state

These are taxable but paid without tax deducted. This includes the basic state pension, the State Earnings Related Pension Scheme (SERPS), the graduated pension (for employees who paid National Insurance under the scheme at any time between April 1961 and April 1975) and non-contributory retirement pension (a top-up pension for those aged 80 who qualify).

State pensions paid to a married women count as her income for tax purposes even if the pension is paid because of her husband's National Insurance contributions. But an adult dependency addition paid to a husband in respect of his wife counts as his income.

Give your tax office a month's warning before drawing your state pension, and tell it what income you expect to earn after you retire. If you work past state pension age and pay tax through PAYE, you will receive a new coding notice. If you're self-employed, you'll need to fill out a self-assessment form.

You are exempt from National Insurance contributions after state pension age. Form CF384 to an employer proves you are exempt and is sent to you when you claim your pension. If you defer your state pension and carry on working, get the form from the DSS.

Pensions from a former employer

These normally have tax deducted under PAYE. You might think your pension is being taxed at a higher rate than your earnings before retirement. But tax is probably being collected on other taxable income, notably the state pension.

Pensions from a personal plan

These normally have tax deducted under PAYE. Pensions from older-style retirement annuity contracts taken out before July 1988 usually have basic-rate tax deducted. Higher-rate taxpayers will have extra tax to pay. Non-taxpayers and those whose top rate is 20 per cent tax will have some tax to claim back.

Annuities

Those bought with your own money (purchased life annuities) have a tax-free 'capital element'. Annuities from pension schemes or plans (compulsory purchase annuities) are fully taxable. A purchased life annuity can be bought with the tax-free lump sum from a pension plan or scheme.

Pensions from abroad

You normally pay tax on nine-tenths of pensions from abroad, even if you don't bring the money into the UK. German and Austrian government pensions paid to UK victims of Nazi persecution are tax-free.

Age-related allowances

Did you or your spouse reach the age of 65 or 75 between and including 6 April 1997 and 5 April 1998? You may qualify for higher allowances: a personal allowance of £5,220 at 65, £5,400 at 75, a married couple's allowance of £3,185 at 65, £3,225 at 75. The extra allowances depend on your total income – gross (before-tax) taxable income, minus some tax-allowable deductions, such as covenanted payments to charity. You lose £1 of the extra allowances for every £2 that your total income exceeds £15,600 in the 1997-8 tax year.

You can claim the higher married couple's allowance if either partner reaches 65 or 75 during the tax year. The extra allowance goes to the husband and is based on his total income, even if he qualifies because of his wife's age (though the basic married couple's allowance can still be transferred to the wife). If his total income exceeds £15,600, his personal allowance is reduced first. Once it is reduced to the basic personal allowance, he starts to lose the extra age-related married couple's allowance.

Keep your income down

If you exceed the total income limit, choose investments carefully. You may be able to keep within the total income limit if, say, you switch to a tax-free investment such as a TESSA, a PEP or National Savings certificates.

If you give to charity regularly, paying by covenant will increase your donations and reduce your total income. For example, covenanting £77 a year to a charity will enable it to claim £23 basic rate tax from the Inland Revenue (at 1997-8 rates of tax). This grossed-up covenant would reduce your total income by £100. But note: savings income is taxed at 20 per cent for basic-rate taxpayers. If you pay a charitable covenant from savings income, you could be billed for the difference – 3 per cent – between the tax you pay on savings and the 23 per cent rate the charity will be able to reclaim.

For one-off payments of at least £250 (after tax) to charity, the Gift Aid scheme is also useful.

DEALING WITH THE INLAND REVENUE

The Taxpayer's Charter commits the Inland Revenue to the principles of helpfulness, courtesy, fairness and confidentiality, and covers your right of appeal against its decisions. The Charter also reminds you of your legal duty to disclose all necessary information.

The Charter is backed up by Inland Revenue codes of practice. For example, *Code of Practice 1* 'Mistakes by the Inland Revenue' states that if the Revenue delays in replying to a query for more than six months (beyond its 28-day target), it will waive interest on any tax you owe, pay interest on any refund due, and pay reasonable costs incurred because of the delay.

When the Inland Revenue makes mistakes you may be entitled to compensation. Tax may be waived if the Revenue is late in asking you for it. If the mistake is serious, it will pay reasonable costs you incur, such as postage and professional fees, as well as earnings you lost through having to sort things out. Even if mistakes aren't serious, but the Revenue persists in making them, it may pay some costs.

Problem-solving

If you have a problem – for example you think too much tax is being deducted or that your allowances are wrong, ring your tax office or local tax enquiry centre to check the rules. Get it to say exactly which rules it thinks apply. When you contact your tax inspector, give your name, National Insurance number and tax reference number. Take a note of the tax inspector's name. Keep copies of letters.

- If you pay tax under PAYE, your tax office may be a long distance from where you live or work. Details of your tax affairs can be sent to a local office so that you can talk to staff there. Look under 'Inland Revenue' in the phone book for your nearest local tax office or tax enquiry centre.
- If you meet with delay, rudeness, maladministration or incompetence, consult the Taxpayer's Charter. More than six weeks' delay is worth complaining about.
- If you're getting nowhere, write to the officer-in-charge at your tax office, whose name is on tax office letters. Head your letter 'complaint'.
- If you're still dissatisfied, write to the regional controller for the area responsible for your tax office. Your tax office will tell you how.
- If you can't resolve the problem, try the Adjudicator. See the Adjudicator's leaflet *How to Complain about the Inland Revenue*. Phone 0171-930 2292 or write to Revenue Adjudicator's Office, Haymarket House, 28 Haymarket, London SW1Y 4SP. The Adjudicator won't deal with matters investigated (or still under investigation) by the Parliamentary Ombudsman.

Penalties

If you don't send the 1997-8 return back by 31 January 1999, you will be charged a fixed penalty of £100. If the tax return is still outstanding six months later, you will be charged a further £100. A further penalty of up to £60 a day can be applied in more serious cases.

If you're late paying your tax, you will be charged interest. In addition, a 5 per cent surcharge will be applied on any tax not paid by 28 February 1999. This surcharge will be increased to 10 per cent if tax is still unpaid by 31 July 1999. The Revenue can start legal proceedings to enforce collection of overdue tax.

Even if you use a tax adviser or accountant to complete your return, you are legally responsible for the accuracy of the information sent and meeting deadlines. Appeal against the penalties and surcharges if you think you have a reasonable case – see Inland Revenue booklets *SA/BK6* and *SA/BK7*. And claim against your accountant or tax adviser if they are at fault.

Interest

As we went to press, the Revenue levied an interest rate of 9.5 per cent a year and paid out 4.75 per cent.

Paying the tax

- If you are an employee or receive an employer's pension, tax is usually deducted by your employer under the Pay As You Earn (PAYE) scheme. If this applies to you and you also have some untaxed income from another source, you can usually pay the extra tax via PAYE.
- The income from certain types of investment is paid to you net of lower-rate (20 per cent) tax, with no further tax to pay if you're a lower- or basic-rate taxpayer.
- If you have income from self-employment, income from property, or income from savings or investment that is not taxed at source, you will probably have to make two 'payments on account' each year. For the 1997-8 tax year the first payment was due to be paid on 31 January 1998 and the second on 31 July 1998. Any balance of tax due will have to be paid by 31 January 1999, along with the first payment on account for the next tax year.
- For the first year of self-assessment (1996-7), people with only investment and/or property income were asked to make a single payment of tax on 31 January 1997. From the 1997-8 tax year onwards, these taxpayers also have to make two payments – one on 31 January and one on 31 July.

Payments on account: how much?

Each payment on account is normally half your tax liability for the previous tax year, *excluding* tax deducted at source and capital gains tax. So if your liability for

1997-8 were £5,400, you would need to pay £2,700 on 31 January 1999 and £2,700 on 31 July 1999 on account for the 1998-9 tax year. But you can reduce the payments you make on account if, for example:

- you know your business profits or rent or savings or investment income will be less during 1998-9 than it was during 1997-8
- you have more tax allowances or tax reliefs
- you have more tax deducted at source.

If your final tax turns out to be more than you anticipated, you will be charged interest on the underpayment from the date the payment of account was due – 31 January or 31 July. By contrast, if you make the payments on account requested and they turn out to be too high, you will receive interest on the overpayments.

Taxpayers who calculate their own tax bills
Put a figure for your first payment on account in box 18.6 of your tax return and in the tax calculation working sheet accompanying the 1997-8 tax return. Tick box 18.7 on the tax return if you want to reduce payments on account. Estimate the tax you expect to pay for 1998-9 and make each payment on account half this amount. Put the amount you want to pay in box 18.6. Explain why you have reduced the payments under the 'additional information' section of your return.

The Revenue checks for simple errors or miscalculations. The Revenue will send a correction notice with an explanation of any corrections if necessary. Contact the Revenue straight away if you don't understand or disagree. You are entitled to have the figures in your return restored, or you can make your own correction. Once your 1997-8 liability has been corrected your tax office will send you your statement of account.

If the Revenue calculates your tax bill

You will receive a statement of account. It will show your total liability for the 1997-8 tax year, how any underpayment will be collected or overpayment refunded, and payments on account due for the 1998-9 tax year. If you don't understand how the figures have been calculated or disagree with them, contact your tax office straight away. Just before the first payment on account is due, you will receive a statement of account with a payment slip for 31 January 1999, the first payment date.

You can reduce payments on account using claim form SA303, sent with your statement of account. It asks you to confirm what payments on account you wish to make, and why you are reducing them. You should complete this and return it to your tax office.

When payments on account don't apply

Is the tax you owe £500 or less? Or is at least 80 per cent of your total income taxed at source? If either applies, there are no payments on account. Instead, you make one payment of the tax due on 31 January following the end of the tax year. Alternatively, the Revenue will collect the tax via your PAYE code if the tax you owe is £1,000 or less *and* you file your tax return by 30 September after the tax year.

Normally, statements of account are sent only to tax-payers who make payments on account. Other taxpayers will receive a notice (a calculation statement) from their tax office only if their return is incorrect, or the tax calculation is wrong.

Paying the wrong amount of tax

If you have overpaid tax because of a mistake you made on your tax return, you can claim a rebate up to six years later. If you tell your tax office before 6 April 1999 you can go back to the 1992-3 tax year. If you overpaid tax because of a mistake by the Inland Revenue or other government department, you can go back 20 years and may be entitled to compensation. If you discover an error, see Inland Revenue leaflet *Code of Practice 1*.

The Inland Revenue will either return overpaid tax by cheque or offset the overpayment against other tax you owe. You normally get interest on your refund from the date of the overpayment. You can claim your tax refund on your tax return (box Q19). If you do not get a tax return, ask your tax office for advice. It may send you form R40, the form used to make a claim for a tax refund.

You may have paid too little tax if your payments on account plus tax deducted at source added up to less than your total tax bill, or you did not disclose all your income for the year, or your circumstances changed and you received allowances in your PAYE code to which you were not entitled.

Where relevant, the Revenue will give you a statement of account showing the up-to-date tax position. It will show any tax due by 31 January 1999. Challenge the statement if you think it is incorrect. If you pay late, the Inland Revenue will charge interest from the date the tax was due.

Enquiries

The Inland Revenue can open an enquiry into a tax return that seems to be incorrect or incomplete – for example, because of previous tax records. It also enquires into some 8,000 returns selected at random. A 'full' enquiry looks into the whole return; an 'aspect' enquiry concentrates on one or more aspects of it (for example, the amount paid to pension schemes, or the calculation of a capital gain). The Revenue must:

- tell you in writing that it intends to start an enquiry
- tell you what your rights and responsibilities are
- try to tell you at the same time the information it requires or, if it can't do this at the outset, it must explain why and say when you can expect to be told
- allow you to be professionally represented if you wish.

The Revenue must tell you within 12 months of the final filing date (or the date you submit your return, if later) if it intends to start an enquiry. The final filing date for the 1997-8 tax year is 31 January 1999. For more information, see Inland Revenue *Code of Practice 11*.

Challenging changes to your tax bill

Has your tax bill been amended following an enquiry?

- The Revenue must explain why it has made the amendment. If you do not understand, ask your tax office to explain the calculations in more detail.
- If you disagree with the amendment or with any other assessment the Revenue makes, you can appeal within 30 days of the date you are advised of the amendment. (See leaflet *IR37* for more information.)
- If you cannot reach agreement with your tax office after lodging the appeal, you can appeal to independent appeal commissioners. General commissioners deal with most cases. Special commissioners deal with cases requiring expertise – you may request that your case be heard by one of these. You can be represented by, for example, a lawyer, accountant or tax specialist (such as a member of the Chartered Institute of Taxation). This can be expensive but may make the difference between winning and losing.
- If you disagree with the commissioners' decision on a point of fact, there is normally no further appeal, but you can complain about maladministration by the Revenue if applicable.
- If you disagree with the commissioners' decision on a point of law, you can take your case to the High Court in England and Wales (the Court of Session in Scotland or the Court of Appeal in Northern Ireland). Tell the commissioners' clerk in writing within 30 days, enclosing £25. Consider the possible costs of this route, along with the interest building up on any tax due.

Keeping records

All taxpayers are obliged to keep records to support the information given on the tax return. Employees and pensioners should keep records such as P60s, mileage records, bank statements and dividend vouchers at least until 31 January 2000 for the 1997-8 tax year. People with savings or investments should keep dividend vouchers, interest statements and so on for the same length of time.

Self-employed taxpayers, or those with rental income, should keep details of expenses, goods purchased and sold, account books and so on until at least 31 January 2004 for the 1997-8 tax year. It's a good idea to keep documents about personal accounts, too, in case you need to establish what transfers did or did not take place between business and personal accounts.

For more information, see Inland Revenue booklets *SA/BK3*, *SA/BK4* and *SA/BK8*.

INDEX

abroad
  income from 26
  pensions from 79
accommodation, low-rent and
  rent-free 42, 60
accrued income 14
additional personal allowance
  28, 34, 68, 69, 71, 72
adoption allowances 16
age-related allowances 8, 15,
  28, 35, 79–80
annuities 79

benefits in kind *see* fringe
  benefits
betting winnings and lottery
  prizes 16
blind person's allowance 28, 67
building society interest 27

canteen meals 39
capital allowances 52–3
  short-life assets 52–3
  writing-down allowance 52
capital gains 17, 26
capital gains tax 9, 73, 84
cars
  authorised mileage rates 46
  capital allowances 53
  company cars 13, 20, 43–5
  Fixed Profit Car Scheme
  (FPCS) 45–6

  own car 20, 45–6
  running costs 20, 44
  self-employed persons 56
charitable donations 8, 27, 33,
  80
checking your income tax
  (calculator) 21–8
children
  child care 39, 54–5
  maintenance payments 74,
    75, 76
  personal allowance 69
  trust income 70
coding notice 32–5
  allowances 33, 35
  code letters 35–6
  deductions 34–5
  restricted allowances 34
company cars 13, 20, 43–5
  classic cars 43
  fuel charges 45
  pool cars 45
  taxable value 43–4
  two cars 44–5
company vans 41
compensation payments 16
council tax and rent rebates 16
covenants 27, 80

debit and credit cards 42
divorce *see* separation and
  divorce

double taxation relief 26

education grants and
    scholarships 16
employees
    absences from work 31–2
    changing jobs 30
    directors 10, 38, 40
    first job 32
    fringe benefits 34, 37–46
    more than one job 13, 30,
        36
    part-time earnings,
        commission and tips 34
    PAYE (Pay As You Earn)
        29–33, 84
    stopping work 30–1
    work-related expenses
        18–20, 33
entertainment 19–20, 39, 57

fees and subscriptions 8, 19,
    33, 38
fringe benefits 34, 37–46
    company cars 13, 20, 43–5
    directors 38
    tax-free 38–40
    taxable 40–6
    taxable value 37
    threshold 37–8

gifts 39, 73
goods, free and discounted 39,
    42

home
    letting 60, 61–5

mortgages see mortgages
    sale of 17
    separation and 72
    working at or from 20
home improvement grants 16
housing benefit 16

income
    gross 21, 27
    taxable 21, 26, 28
    total 21
income tax 7, 9, 47
inheritance tax 9, 73
Inland Revenue 81–90
    challenging tax bills 85–6,
        88–9
    enquiries 10, 88
    helpline 13
    mistakes by 81
    penalties 83
    problems and complaints
        81–2
    tax calculation 86
    tax calculation guides 26
insurance benefits 14, 16, 26,
    27, 38
interest
    from savings and
        investments 14, 16, 34, 84
    on overdue tax 83, 85, 88
    on tax rebates 16, 85, 87
investment income 14, 16, 34,
    35, 61, 84
    joint investments 68

loans 20, 41, 58
    see also mortgages

luncheon vouchers 39

maintenance payments 16, 33, 34, 72, 73–6
marriage 66–9
   death of a spouse 67–8
   joint investment income 68
   and mortgage tax relief 68–9
   tax allowances 66–7, 69, 71–2
   see also separation and divorce
married couple's allowance 8, 28, 34, 66, 67, 71, 72
maternity allowance and pay 32
medical insurance 34, 41
MIRAS 17, 59–60
mobile phones 41
mortgages
   joint borrowers 59
   letting your home 60, 65
   MIRAS 17, 59–60
   outside MIRAS 33, 34, 60
   tax relief 26, 41, 59–60
   tax relief, arrears and 60
   tax relief and married couples 68–9, 72

National Insurance 36, 47–8, 55, 78
National Savings interest 34

older people 77–80
   age-related allowances 8, 15, 28, 79–80
   keeping income down 80

pensions *see* pensions

P9D 37
P11D 10, 37
P45 30, 31
P46 32
P50 31
P60 9, 17, 18, 29
P60U 31
parking costs 40
partnerships 11–12, 47
PAYE (Pay As You Earn) 29–33, 84
   coding notice 32–5
   emergency code 30, 32
   PAYE code 29–30
   reference number 16
payment of tax
   over– and underpayments 10, 26, 30, 34–5, 85, 87
   payments on account 9, 10, 84–5, 86–7
   see also PAYE
pensions 8
   annuities 79
   employer's pension schemes 9, 18, 38, 78
   exempt pensions 14–15
   from abroad 79
   FSAVC schemes 33
   personal pension plans 9, 13, 26, 33, 78
   SERPS 77
   state pensions 34, 77–8
PEPs 7, 18
personal allowance 8, 28, 35, 66

personal injury damages 16
private residence relief 17
prizes 40
protective or functional clothing
    19, 39, 58

records, keeping 90
redundancy counselling
    services 40
redundancy pay 16, 26
reference books and stationery
    19
removal and relocation
    expenses 39
rental income 34, 61–5, 84
    allowable expenses 64–5
    business trading income 63
    holiday lettings 63–4
    losses 65
    rent-a-room scheme 62–3,
        65
    services, provision of 65
    tax relief on mortgage
        interest 65
    taxation 61

schedules 8
self-employment 47–58, 84
    allowable expenses 54–8
    business rates 48
    capital allowances 52–3
    closing down 51
    first year 49–50
    income tax 47
    keeping records 90
    limited companies 47
    losses 53

National Insurance 47–8, 55
    overlap profits 50
    self-employed status 48–9
    tax return 12, 13
    taxable profits 51–2
    VAT (Value Added Tax) 48,
        54
separation and divorce 71–6
    and capital gains tax 73
    and inheritance tax 73
    maintenance payments 16,
        33, 34, 72, 73–6
    and mortgage interest tax
        relief 72
    tax allowances 71–2
shares 17, 27
sick pay 31–2
social security benefits 7, 16,
    30–1, 32, 34
sports facilities 40
staff functions 39
subsistence 40, 56–7

tax allowances
    additional personal
        allowance 28, 34, 68,
        69, 71, 72
    age-related allowances 8,
        15, 28, 35, 79–80
    blind person's allowance
        28, 67
    claiming 15
    married couple's allowance
        8, 28, 34, 66, 67, 71, 72
    personal allowance 8, 28,
        35, 66
    transfer of 66, 67

widow's bereavement
    allowance 28, 34, 67
tax evasion 8
tax-free income 7, 16, 80
tax rates
    capital gains tax 9
    income tax 9
    inheritance tax 9
tax rebates 16, 30–1, 32, 87
tax return 9, 10
    completion 11–20
    computer generated 15
    errors, avoiding 12–15
    photocopies 15
    rounding figures up and
        down 13–14
    signing and dating 15
    standard tax return 11

supplementary pages 12
    tax calculation 85–6
Taxpayer's Charter 81, 82
TESSAs 7, 18
timetable 9–10
tools and instruments 8, 19
top-slicing relief 26
training courses 18–19, 40
travel costs 20, 40, 56–7
travel and other vouchers 42
trust income 18, 70

unmarried couples 71

VAT (Value Added Tax) 48, 54

widow's bereavement
    allowance 28, 34, 67

Here's just a flavour of some of the reports planned for future issues of *Which?*

- Water supplies • Holiday money • Car warranties • Contact lenses
- Internet service providers • Fridge freezers • Mortgage advice
- Cutting fuel bills • Small family cars • International phone calls
- Endowments • Sending money abroad • Buying a cooker
- Hiring a car abroad • Private medical insurance

So why not take up our trial offer today?

SUMMARY OF OFFER

3 free issues of Which? as they are published • Just fill in the delayed direct debiting instruction below and post it to Which?, FREEPOST, Hertford X, SG14 1YB • If you do not wish to continue beyond the free trial period simply write to us at the address above, and to your Bank/Building Society to cancel your direct debiting instruction, before the 1st payment is due • Your first payment will be due on the 1st of the month 3 months after the date you sign the mandate (so for example, if you sign the mandate on 15th August, your 1st payment is due on 1st November) • No action is necessary if you wish to continue after the free trial. We will send you Which? each month for the current price of £14.75 a quarter, until you cancel or until we advise you of a change in price • We would give you at least 6 weeks notice in advance of any change in price, so you would have plenty of time to decide whether to continue – you are of course free to cancel at any time.

Offer subject to acceptance. Which? Ltd, Reg in England Reg No 677665. Reg Office 2 Marylebone Road, London NW1 4DF. Reg under the Data Protection Act. As result of responding to this offer, your name and address might be added to a mailing list. This could be used by ourselves (Which? Ltd, or our parent company Consumers' Association) or other companies for sending you offers in the future. If you prefer not to receive such offers, please write to Dept DNP3 at the above Hertford address or tick the box on the coupon if you only want to stop offers from other companies. You will not be sent any future offers for 5 years, in compliance with the British Code of Advertising and Sales Promotion.

▼ DETACH HERE ▼

Your name and address in BLOCK CAPITALS PLEASE

Name (Mr/Mrs/Miss/Ms)	Address
	Postcode

To: Which?, FREEPOST, Hertford X, SG14 1YB

Please send me the next 3 months' issues of Which? magazine as they appear. I understand that I am under no obligation – if I do not wish to continue after the 3 months' free trial, I can cancel my order before my first payment is due on the 1st of the month 3 months after the date I sign the mandate. But if I decide to continue I need do nothing – my subscription will bring me monthly Which? for the current price of £14.75 a quarter.

Direct Debiting Instruction Please pay Which? Ltd Direct Debits from the account detailed on this Instruction subject to the safeguards assured by The Direct Debit Guarantee. I understand that this Instruction may remain with Which? and if so, details will be passed electronically to any bank or building society.

_DB9_W

Signed   Date

Bank/Building Society account in the name of

Name and address of your Bank/Building Society in BLOCK CAPITALS PLEASE

To:

*Banks/Building Societies may decline to accept Direct Debits to certain types of account other than current accounts

*Bank/Building Society Acct. No.

Bank/Building Society Sort Code

Tick here if you do not wish to receive promotional mailings from other companies ☐

Postcode

NO STAMP NEEDED • SEND NO MONEY